On Resilience

Writers in the *On Series*

Elisabeth Wynhausen

On Resilience

hachette
AUSTRALIA

Every attempt has been made to locate the copyright holders for
material quoted in this book. Any person or organisation that may
have been overlooked or misattributed may contact the publisher.

Published in Australia and New Zealand in 2020
by Hachette Australia
(an imprint of Hachette Australia Pty Limited)
Level 17, 207 Kent Street, Sydney NSW 2000
www.hachette.com.au

First published in 2009 by Melbourne University Publishing

10 9 8 7 6 5 4 3 2 1

A catalogue record for this
book is available from the
National Library of Australia

ISBN: 978 0 7336 4436 8 (paperback)

Original cover concept by Nada Backovic Design
Text design by Alice Graphics
Typeset by Typeskill
Printed and bound in Australia by McPherson's Printing Group

The paper this book is printed on is certified against the
Forest Stewardship Council® Standards. McPherson's Printing
Group holds FSC® chain of custody certification SA-COC-005379.
FSC® promotes environmentally responsible, socially beneficial
and economically viable management of the world's forests.

The year after the cycling accident that left my brother Jules badly brain-damaged, I loaded him and his wheelchair into my car one Sunday, got in and cautiously asked him how he was feeling. His old self might have said something like 'How the fuck do you think I feel?' He had taught English as a young man; now if he were prodded with questions, he mumbled a few indistinct phrases. He had been a constant reader but now held books up in front of him, going through the motions, without turning a page. He had loved travelling and, being adept at languages, had learnt to speak Italian the year he went to Italy with his wife, and Spanish when they went to Spain. He had been contented at home; now he was in a nursing home that always smelled faintly of piss and shit. He knew who we were, but not, in a sense, who he was or what he had become. Though one might mistake his withdrawn impassivity—one of the effects of the damage to the frontal lobes—for a shadowy residue of his former self, there were traces of his old sense of humour and his stoicism, especially if he were asked how he felt about his situation. '*C'est la vie*', he said.

We had grown up in a family in which resilience was taken for granted, as if fortitude in the face of adversity was nothing special, though my mother, who personified it, didn't mind being reminded of her more teeth-clenching feats of endurance, like the time she fractured her kneecap, tripping over one of the garments she had just picked up from a clothing manufacturer in the city. A passer-by helped her to her car, and she drove herself back to her dress shop in Sydney's northern suburbs. There was an echo of the same refusal to succumb to mere catastrophe in my brother's words, but it was just that: an echo of the resolute realism that was part of our heritage.

The outlines of the story traced something of the same course as the stories of many others who settled in Australia, whether the nineteenth-century Irish or the twenty-first-century Sudanese. My mother and father had left their homeland once in fear of their lives, and once to start over, in a country they knew so little about they pictured themselves on a farm with a couple of meadows with bright green grass and gnarled old apple and pear trees, like the farm we had just left behind, in a village in the south of Holland. It had been my mother's home for only a few years, but she had quickly adapted to its demands, just as she had adapted during the tumultuous years that preceded it and would adapt to the hardships that followed, both in the first years in Australia and the last, more than half a century later.

Her death in 2007, at the age of ninety-two, prompted me to consider what it was that kept her going, against all odds. It gave me an excuse for celebrating her life, in light of the feeling, common to my generation, that our parents were a great deal more durable than we could ever hope to be and that our children and grandchildren will be less durable than we are, as if the resilience often thought to define earlier generations is petering out. But being able to absorb the blows doesn't explain the essential component of resilience—the resistance that determines a person's capacity to bounce back from traumatic events—a process now often acclaimed as a key to success in personal and commercial life that anyone can learn, through the right sort of thinking. If that is the case, then mum gave a demonstration of resilience exemplary in its simplicity, because she had the knack of making the best of life, however difficult its circumstances.

Born in 1915, my mother Marianne, whose family called her Nanny, belonged to the generation that came of working age during the Depression, in an era most women were denied education; already at work in the family butchery by the age of fourteen, as her father wished, she insisted on going to night school to study bookkeeping and French. Speaking the language would help save her life during the war, but such thoughts were far from her mind at the age of nineteen, when she briefly left home because her parents had forbidden her from seeing her boyfriend, a distant cousin. She had found work and lodgings in a nearby town before she let the family know where she was—an early sign of the strong-mindedness that would become like the sinews of her resilience. Though soon back with the family, by the late thirties she was in Scheveningen, a holiday town on the North Sea, working as a shop assistant in a department store that got a very stylish summer crowd, at least according to my mother, whose fond memories had turned Scheveningen, with its grey sea and its grey sky, into a picture-perfect model of glamour that rivalled prewar Biarritz or Monte Carlo. It has to be said there were periods when she didn't see much of it. In winter, the shopgirls started work before it was light and finished work after it was dark. But even the routines of those strange, ominous years before the war could be savoured in retrospect, in the knowledge that it was all about to be snatched away.

Back in Arnhem again in May 1940, when the columns of German troops invading the Netherlands marched into the city (and the country) across the bridge over the Rhine, their footsteps hammering through nearby streets, she fled in 1942, with her brother Nico and a friend, after her mother urged them to go, fearing that the often impulsive Nico would otherwise be picked up and deported.

Long afterwards, my mother would recall being in a small town in occupied France when the air-raid sirens sounded. Forced to take shelter a little way from the café where she was meeting up again with Nico and their friend Dolf, she dived into a cellar and found herself surrounded by German soldiers. They tried to talk to her. My mother pretended to cry. 'It was terrible', she told me. 'I had reason to cry, but it's hard to keep it up for two hours.' Mum's brisk humour said as much about her as her lack of self-pity, but if these aspects of her temperament reinforced her resilience, the resourcefulness—the smarts—that allowed her to come up with the solution to her problem is closer to its essence. I wouldn't dream of saying her ingenuity under pressure was what saved her life, however. Leaving her homeland behind saved her life. There were 140 000 Jews in the Netherlands at the outbreak of war. One hundred and seven thousand were deported, and all but 5000 of them were murdered by the Nazis, three of my grandparents and many of my parents' aunts, uncles and cousins among them.

Books on the subject of resilience often cite concentration camp survivor Viktor Frankl, a Viennese psychiatrist who wrote about his experiences in *Man's Search for Meaning*, suggesting that those who survived the camps had exerted the only form of control they could over their lives, finding meaning even in their suffering rather than succumbing to the horrors around them. One hesitates to pivot about the words of a man of great moral authority who survived Theresienstadt (where his father died) and Auschwitz (where his mother and brother were murdered) and went on to write a classic hailed long afterwards as one of the ten most influential books in the USA. But large numbers of very resilient people died in the gas chambers, and countless more resilient people died from shelling, bombing, starvation and disease in the course of a war usually estimated to have cost the lives of about thirty million civilians and more than twenty million military personnel—something that must surely be said before one can speculate about the attributes that combined with luck to spare the lives of others.

It was often sheer chance, of course— the same shocking fortuitousness that drove our ancestors into the arms of religion (searching for meaning, as Frankl would). You might live if you didn't look too 'Jewish', or die if you did. Or live because you took one road and not another, or because you made a decision about whether or not to trust someone, as my mother did, after she, Nico and Dolf were arrested by a couple of German soldiers soon after crossing the border. Taken to a nearby French post and interviewed by a local policeman because she was fluent in French, my mother decided to trust him, confiding that in Holland she had helped escaped French prisoners of war, providing clothes and money, which were passed on through their contacts in the underground. She could have been shot there and then. But she had made the right decision. The doors of the cells and the building were left open that night as the cop had promised and they got away.

If asked to explain her instinctive response, my mother would have looked blank, which wasn't like her. Her decision had been the right one, after all, and like many resilient people, she wasn't one to keep wondering how to categorise her experiences, or if she had been luckier or unluckier than most; she was more likely to be thinking about what would have to be done next. Resilient people always see a way of coping, and if the first thing they try doesn't work, they try a bunch of other things, says a psychiatrist I know, applying a no-nonsense definition that is like a tonic, especially now resilience gets passed off as something constituted out of sentiments that could be stitched on a sampler, with slogans like 'Face up to problems' or 'Learn from bad times' substituting for the grittiness at its core.

Before they had even slipped over the Dutch frontier, my mother had tricked a man who had agreed to change their Dutch guilders into French francs but had come back threatening to expose them unless they gave him more money. They had very little for the perilous journey ahead. My mother was carrying a small basket with a change of clothes, a brush, a comb and a mirror. There was only one other thing: with a great show of reluctance and a look of hurt innocence in her blue eyes, she gave the man the ring from her finger. He was persuaded it was valuable. It might have been once, but she had lost the stones in the ring and had them replaced with worthless copies, she told me many years later. By that time she was drawn to pursuits that involved calculated risks, another trait that gets honourable mention in the fast-growing body of literature on the subject of resilience. But when we spoke about the war, it was her brother's actions, not her own, that she identified as risk-taking, as if discounting the risks she had taken because she was confident of her own judgement, a trait that is also very much a part of the personality profile of many resilient people

The three found themselves at one point in a French town that had a curfew at night. Not knowing what to do next, Nico acted on a hunch, speaking to a butcher in a bar, mustering enough French to say that he was a butcher too, and that he and the people with him were in trouble. 'It was a very risky thing to do—the butcher was drunk', my mother recalled. But the man took them home. 'His wife started screaming at him, but when he said he had Dutch refugees with him, his wife took us upstairs and fed us.' In the morning, she made them packs of sandwiches, and he led them to the train, got their tickets and showed them where to sit to avoid inspection, which they did, by the skin of their teeth.

My grandmother had stayed in Holland because her mother had refused to move out of her own house. The old lady had already been murdered, I believe, when the people sheltering my grandmother Elisabeth were betrayed; she died in the gas chambers at Sobibor, a death camp in south-eastern Poland. Her death was seldom far from my mother's mind, but she hardly ever spoke of it. On the rare occasions my parents did mention the war, they spoke instead of the lively goings-on around them. In Switzerland, where they met and married, they had been interned with an assortment of refugees that included circus performers, cabaret artistes and a Dutchwoman with a title, who figured in a story we may not have heard as children since it began with my mother walking into a room where four people were in bed together, doing anything but brooding over the terrible things going on elsewhere.

By the spring of 1945, not long before VE Day, my mother had returned to Holland and had moved into the farmhouse in Heer where several generations of my father's family had lived. He had been called up, joining a Dutch brigade then serving with the British forces under

Montgomery. My mother had a Colt .45 revolver dad had got hold of; while she couldn't imagine firing it, it gave her some comfort to sleep with it under her pillow, since she wasn't alone in the house. The place had been occupied by a man by the name of Kusters; his wartime activities got him gaoled as a collaborator but hadn't deterred the municipal authorities from signing the farm over to him, a reminder that the Dutch, like the Germans, were meticulous record keepers—as historians of the Holocaust have noted in explaining why such a high percentage of Dutch Jews were located and murdered. The records were only part of it, of course. While many ordinary citizens risked their lives to hide Jewish people from the Nazis, two-thirds of them were rounded up along with the Jews they were hiding, evidence of the fact that it wasn't unusual for other ordinary Dutch citizens like Kusters to collaborate with the Nazis. He was already locked up but his wife and some of her unsavoury friends were still in the house, entertaining American soldiers in the front rooms, when my mother moved in upstairs. She had the key to the front door but she didn't have the piece of paper from the *burgemeester* she needed to get the house back, and for the next six weeks she went to the council day after day to talk to officials, standing up to them until the paper was in her hand and the Kusters woman was gone at last.

The house had been stripped, but there were still cows on the farm. The rule stipulating that all the milk had to go to the authorities seemed to have been made to be broken by my mother. Now resilience gets such a good press, its promoters tend to gloss over another tendency: the flexibility that allows resilient people to view problems from different perspectives may also make them a little too inventive in finding solutions. I should hastily add that all my mother did was to keep some milk back and make butter on the sly at night. It amused her later in life to recall that in the months before my father came back home, she furnished the house out of the black-market butter and preserved fruits she traded for sheets and pillowcases, dishes, plates, knives, forks, spoons—even the preserving jars for the black-market fruit—with the highly respectable department store Vroom & Dreesman, which had a branch in nearby Maastricht.

Recalling details from those days—like the sound of the dogcart over the cobbled street that woke her up at five in the morning when two boys from the village came to do the milking—she would steer clear of the obvious question: how had she kept herself going when she was also coping with overwhelming feelings of grief and loss? This is surely the question at the heart of any consideration of resilience. My mother would have found the immediate hardships a welcome distraction.

Moreover, she was doing something particularly purposeful by reassembling the farmhouse, putting the pieces of something back together again when so much else had been shattered. She was likely to be calculating how many kilos of butter would have to be churned to get some more of the white Mosa dinner plates or a soup tureen, or allowing herself some moments of satisfaction at the sight of a cupboard already half-full of china. It was in her nature to focus on what had to be done, an approach associated with resilient people; indeed, when my father was home again, it was his distress that claimed attention, if only indirectly. He had gone back to cattle dealing, which is what his family had done before the war, but he couldn't adapt. He drank too much and got into fights with people known to have been collaborators, who were back in their old jobs as if nothing had happened. My father didn't examine his feelings, then or at any other time in his life. He was devoted to his wife; he wouldn't have known what you were talking about if you suggested that she had been denied support because she was the stronger one. But her body showed the strain. The doctor she consulted about her stomach ulcers around that time, telling him a little of what had happened to her and her family, told her to try to forget. Long afterwards, she liked to recall he had also told her she wasn't strong enough to start life over in Australia.

We arrived in 1951, along with two of my mother's three brothers and their wives. My father sold ties, then hats, for David Jones, which was willing to hire immigrants with thick accents, and then he made a little more money delivering coal for a coal merchant. In 1952, after an accident at another job had put him out of action for months, he took over a milk run, buying a truck my mother would use when he got home, loading it up with bolts of the cloth she sold door to door or at the markets, work that had almost nothing to redeem it, except that people could be kind. 'I often said, "my husband's sick", and he was, often', she said in later life when we spoke about a period I remembered chiefly for its delights: my mother managed to turn simple outings into a succession of little adventures, no less thrilling for following a set pattern, like stopping to picnic on hot chips at the edge of the Cooks River when my brother, our cousin and I went to the markets in Wollongong with her in the school holidays. Though mum had to lug the heavy bolts of material between the truck and the market stall, what was being instilled in us at the ages of five, six and seven was that it was natural to make the best of things.

On the other hand, no small part of her resilience sprung from a stubbornly wilful streak that meant, for instance, that in years to come she treated taxes as something that involved a sporting contest between herself and the tax man, but freely gave money away, as if making up her own rules about what she owed society. This was after she opened her dress shop, Paris Frocks, another setting in which she changed the rules on the spur of the moment, making up different prices for different customers, according to the women who worked with her. One remembered my mother going into the curtained-off area at the back of the shop to have a coffee with a customer whose husband was very ill, before getting out the lay-by book to cross off the amount the woman owed, a kindness worth recording not because it was typical, which it was, but because of the complex emotional calculus involved: the experience of people doing it tough resonated with experiences in her own life.

But if her ready compassion was on one side of the ledger, her aptitude for commerce was on the other. She was a curious combination, a soft touch who regarded it as soft-headed to let opportunities slip through your fingers, who for all her own generosity, was aghast at the realisation that both her children lacked her instinct for business. I always thought she could have had an interesting conversation about it with Kerry Packer, a man with some of the same contradictory impulses, who was so resilient he came back from the dead.

But my mother was content in her suburban dress shop. People bought less but expected more social interaction in those days, when the purchase of a new dress or a pair of shoes could be something of an occasion itself. Like the owners of other small shops, my mother knew many of her customers well enough for them to stay for a chat when they dropped in to put ten shillings or a few dollars of the housekeeping money on a lay-by. Paris Frocks was the sort of place where people often went and had a coffee out the back, in fact. There were strong bonds between my mother and several other saleswomen; one would be her closest friend for the rest of her life. Mum was a first-class saleswoman for some of the same reasons she was resilient: her vivacity made people want to go along with her; her enthusiasm was contagious, and she had the happy knack of matching garments to customers. But by chance she had employed one person as reticent as she was forthcoming: even if customers were leaving empty-handed after trying on clothes for an hour, that woman would meekly say 'very well, then' as they slipped out the door, making my mother bridle however often she heard it. She could stand almost anything but the waste of a good customer. Her own capacity to capitalise on the moment convinced her anyone could be coaxed to try one thing more, even if it was only a plastic necklace dangling from the little jewellery stand on the front counter, or the clip-on earrings that had appeared like magic in her hands.

But the playfulness said to be a characteristic of resilient people could get the better of her. One day a customer brought

back a nylon dress she had worn to a function the night before, burning a small hole
in it, probably with ash from her cigarette.
Pointing out this imperfection, she said
they should take the dress back. It was clear
she had only wanted the garment for the
one night, and my mother told her she'd
get her money back if she could see where
the hole had been after they mended it.
When the woman came back, she couldn't
spot the mend, delighting my mother no
end. She had always loved a bet. In later
years she was in a betting syndicate with
a bunch of eighty-somethings, but her
interest in horseracing paled beside her
lasting fascination with the stock market.
I'm not sure when my mother started
buying and selling shares, but until the

last month of her life, she would happily spend hours studying the financial pages and consulting the Bloomberg channel on pay television. The fact that it was how she supported herself in her retirement was a useful smokescreen. The truth was that she relished the game.

Leaving aside some technical variants to do with the snap of steel braces and the springiness of rubber seals, the meanings of the word *resilience* have stayed more or less constant since it sprang into being on the back of the verb *resile*, a word now only used by politicians and lawyers saying they won't (although in English, according to my *Shorter Oxford*, the term *resile* has meant virtually the same thing—springing back or recoiling—for some five hundred years). But *resilience* has suddenly slipped its moorings. The word is being redefined ever more rapidly, the speed of the process matched by the vehemence of the claims, as resilience is endorsed as the cure for everything from damaged children and crumbling communities to moribund, badly managed companies. That puts it in the frame right now, as boom turns to bust and the darkest of premonitions about the financial crisis are realised. The world's financial systems are permeated with toxic subprime mortgages, repackaged as 'assets' by financial institutions that have so thoroughly entangled equity in debt that the consequent credit freeze only starts to set the scene for the hard times ahead. One thing is easy to predict: many chief executives will do first what they used to do last, retrenching armies of workers, adding to miseries that will test the claims made for resilience to the limits.

For hundreds of years, resilience was thought of as something some people had more of than others. These days its promoters insist it is hard-wired in the species—or, as they say, 'normative': 'Resilience is a normative process of human adaptation, encoded in the human species'.[1] In her book *Resilience*, author and broadcaster Anne Deveson observes that by the 1990s scientists regarded resilience as a dynamic process flowing out of the myriad interactions between the person and the environment.[2] 'Intervention to help people develop resilience could occur at any number of places and in any number of ways.' By that time, some psychologists had concluded that their profession's preoccupation with people who were ill or disturbed or unhappy meant psychology was forgetting what there was to be learnt from healthy, fulfilled individuals and thriving communities. The field of positive psychology, as it came to be called, was rooted in the belief that therapy should start with people's strengths, rather than their weaknesses. Norman Garmezy, later emeritus professor of psychology at the University of Minnesota, was among the first to apply the precepts of positive psychology to research into resilience, exploring the elements that helped children from disturbed backgrounds adapt and cope. Instead of looking for ways to stop kids from going under, he started with the ones that didn't and found that children less vulnerable to the stresses and strains of their everyday existence didn't think of themselves as responsible for their parents' mental illness or alcoholism. They probably had a competent, caring adult somewhere in their lives. The countless studies that followed confirmed that resilient children tended to be the ones who were bright, flexible, independent, confident, outgoing, more socially adept, more purposeful and better at solving problems, even as infants. Usually they were more resilient still if they received good care in the first year of their lives and came from families that clung to a semblance of order and set high expectations for the children, although they lived in poverty.

The fact that so many well-intentioned researchers have shown that resilient children cope with continuing stress because they have the qualities we automatically associate with coping alerts us to the shell game that features in the literature on the subject. I'm hardly the first to notice. I had no sooner signed the book contract and Googled the word *resilience* than I discovered I had strayed into a field so crowded that there weren't just thousands of books and papers on the subject; there were also a bunch of meta-studies exploring the tendency to use the word *resilience* so loosely that it sometimes refers to a process, sometimes to the mechanisms that underlie that process, sometimes to the alleged results of that process and sometimes to all three at once. 'When I use a word', Humpty Dumpty tells Alice, 'it means just what I choose it to mean— neither more nor less'. 'The question is', said Alice, 'whether you can make words mean so many different things'.

Resilience, like the hand of God, appears in some incarnations as an intangible but irresistible influence in our lives and in others as a force of nature. Researchers in Hawaii who studied children from troubled households over many years—to find one in three doing okay by the age of eighteen and most doing okay by the time they were in their thirties or forties— spoke of an 'innate self-righting mechanism', a phrase that gained considerable currency, though it stretches the very concept of resilience to mean rebounding *after* fifteen or twenty years, an alarming prospect if we are staring calamity in the face. Of course it makes sense to insist that people can bounce back from hardships of every kind, an idea of great social utility central to the belief that society must do what it can to improve the lives of its most disadvantaged citizens. But the eye-popping claims made for resilience waver between conflicting narratives, dismissing the proposition that some people are hardier than others while invoking stories of heroic resistance to circumstance. Redeemed politicians, therapists and gym-owning jocks alike bandy around the words of the nineteenth-century German philosopher Friedrich Nietzsche: 'What does not destroy me, makes me stronger'. Maybe; maybe not. Nietzsche overcame ill-health to write books that still resonate today, but he went mad at the age of forty-four and never recovered. But lived human experience does not deter the most ardent advocates of the power of positive thinking. Like children at Christmas time, they live in the hope that wishing will make it so, which is why you find qualified professionals with strings of letters after their names earnestly suggesting that suffering humanity will come good, the eyes of the blind opened and the ears of the deaf unstopped, if only enough people are told, 'You have what it takes to get through this'.

The notion that resilience involves thoughts and actions that can be learnt has gone on to inspire everything from PowerPoint presentations on the subject to 'resilience trainers', a whole new subset of smooth talkers trying to make a buck off the proposition that organisations can also be resilient. The way things are going, they will be repackaging honour and loyalty next. With business journals valorising resilience, there are even academic courses in the subject. 'The competitive advantage you can learn', says the blurb for the *two-day* course on 'mental toughness' offered by the University of Auckland Business School. And two days is practically a historical period compared with the transformational forty-nine minutes or so demanded by hypnotherapists flogging CDs containing 'the secret to remaining focused and resilient even in the face of the most challenging circumstances' or something very like it.

That's not to deny that people in extreme situations can surprise themselves with the discovery that they're stronger than they imagined. In recent years, in fact, medical researchers have managed to relate certain changes in the chemistry of the brain to the capacity to function under stress, showing that responses to extreme stress stimulate the production of sub-stances that intensify the level of awareness, regulate fear and spur adaptive behaviour. The fact that resilient people experience lower levels of fear and anxiety in situations outside their control, meanwhile managing to remain more positive and optimistic, can now be underpinned with scientific explanations about the release of adrenal steroids like dehydroepiandros-terone or the rate at which the dopamine neurons are firing. It seems even mice raised in the same litter respond so differently to stress that some become more susceptible while others become more resistant. A study on the subject created headlines in 2007, when scientists found that some mice repeatedly forced into confrontations with larger mice exhibited symptoms of depression and post-traumatic stress disorder. To start with, the smaller animals all showed higher levels of brain-derived-neurotrophic factor, a protein that normally promotes new connections between neurons, apparently helping mice—and men—adapt by learning to recognise and avoid threatening situations. There were differences between the smaller mice thrown back into the situation again and again. More susceptible animals reacted to the continuing stress by overproducing the protein, which made them behave as if the sense of threat had been generalised to other situations, until they were avoiding all other mice and had more or less shut down. Fascinating as it was to be reminded of the many and various ways in which we humans can inflict ourselves on the animal kingdom, it left the real conundrum unexplained. Researchers once again showed how some creatures function so much better under pressure than others without explaining *why*.

The literature on the subject draws on stories the ancients would have recognised because they revolve around epic resistance to tragedy and trauma, fusing timeless themes with the self-help industry's faith in the perfectibility of human nature, but images of everyday life can provide sharper glimpses of the vitality that underpins resilience. At the age of sixty-three—a year older than Agnes

Forbat is when she tells me about him—
her father Miksa could jump from the
ground up onto the cutting table in their
clothing factory, a feat no more notable
than the zest that would prompt so exu-
berantly silly a gesture. Miksa had arrived
in Sydney at the age of forty-six with his
wife and daughter after they fled Hungary
following the Soviet invasion of 1956. All
they had with them was a small overnight
bag with a change of underwear and the
extra set of clothes eleven-year-old Agnes,
the only child, wore one on top of the
other. Relatives in Sydney had advanced
the rent on a small basement flat in Kings
Cross with an outside kitchen and toilet.
They had no money, but three days after

they arrived, Miksa had found a job on the night shift at a flour factory, for fifteen pounds a week. His wife, Ibolya, started taking in sewing.

They had been in Sydney a few months when Ibolya cut her first sample garments, two winter skirts Agnes Forbat can still picture half a century later, from the kick pleat at the back of the black wool gabardine skirt to the satin bow at the top of a small slit pocket. The skirts were packed into a small cardboard box. Agnes, who spoke English by then, remembers her father asking her, 'How do you say "I have some skirts to show you" in English?' Before starting work at the factory, Miksa, a short, balding man no one would have looked at twice, but for the spring in his step, would walk into the city, the cardboard box under his arm, going into all the little dress shops along one side of the street, then the other. Shopkeepers quickly waved him away. It seems his accent made some think he was saying 'I have summer skirts to show you' when the shops were ordering winter things. 'Better luck tomorrow', he'd say when he got home. He was spending his days going from door to door trying to communicate with people he didn't understand and his nights shovelling flour into sacks, before catching a few hours sleep on the sagging sofa—his wife and daughter shared the double bed in the other room. But he was happy. Being in Australia made him feel free, he said. His daughter remembers him as a supremely contented man. That meant he was primed to be resilient.

Laboratory experiments in which people are induced to feel either positive or negative emotions, giving the mice a break, have enlarged on what we might have imagined to be the case, namely that feeling good is good for you and feeling bad isn't. Negative emotions produce increases in heart rate and blood pressure—responses that put people in a state where they may only be able to conceive of actions involving fight or flight. Positive emotions do the opposite, slowing the heart rate and improving a person's ability to notice and process information that bears on the crisis—effects that are amplified over time. People who experience some positive emotions, even while coping with adversity, become more resistant to stress, a pattern that must have set in early in Miksa's case, because life had also taught him to be self-reliant.

One of four sons whose father, a drunk, came and went, Miksa was already busking and selling shoelaces on the streets of Budapest when he was twelve. He started dozens more little businesses, all of which went bankrupt, he later told his daughter. He just kept trying, signalling his willingness to pick himself up and keep going, the objective correlative of resilience. In Sydney, years later, he finally got an order after many weeks when he walked into a shop whose owner spoke German, as he did, because it was his mother's native tongue. It was that language that had helped save his life during the war. Though the Nazis picked him up, he was somehow able to keep getting himself moved from one labour camp to another, in the process seeing most of Europe, as he would tell Agnes. The fact that he survived speaks to his irrepressible ingeniousness and enterprise. How he did so remains a mystery, however. He seldom went into details about what had happened in the past; it was the future that interested him.

In 2002, the *Harvard Business Review* ran an article by Diane Coutu, an editor of the publication, suggesting that resilient people shared three traits—a resolute acceptance of reality, a sense that life is meaningful, and an exceptional ability to improvise—a short list since quoted ad infinitum, not least because it lends itself to the idea that resilience can be acquired.[3] But some do question the assertion that resilient people find meaning in the experience they have risen above. Al Siebert of the Resiliency Centre in Portland, Oregon, observed that in his experience only a very small percentage of the resilient people he had interviewed over the years bothered to verbalise what they had gone through: 'For them it is just something that happened, and they moved past it—without help from therapists or "coaching"'.[4] What that left hanging, so to speak, was the contemporary belief that people have to *process* what they feel before they can move on— the opposite of what many resilient people do. Research has shown that resilient people handle their feelings well, rather than getting all emotional when hit by adversity, said Siebert. Rather than needing a resilience trainer to remind them not to brood over their suffering, they put it behind them to concentrate on the task that lies ahead, an approach they have in common with highly successful people. Contrary to the wisdom being dispensed in short courses on mental toughness, however, there is no inevitable correlation between the two: resilient people like

Miksa Forbat are not necessarily ambitious, finding contentment within their immediate orbit.

Before they left Hungary, Miksa—or Michael—had been in charge of a government department that manufactured nightwear, and Ibolya—Violet—worked on the technical side. They were practical, systematic people who complemented each other, says their daughter. Their first orders in Australia had quickly multiplied. Still eleven years old, Agnes would come home from primary school to write out invoices, make patterns and do the overlocking and finishing while her mother cut layers of fabric or worked at the old treadle sewing machine on the dining table. Before going to sleep, Agnes would pack away the new skirts piled on the double bed. They had few clothes themselves. There was little in the flat but the table, the bed, the sofa, a few chairs and the sewing things. No toys. No records. No television.

These days, when people worry they are softer than their parents and that their children are softer than them, they may be thinking about the fact that the parents made do with less—less stuff, certainly—while the children feel hard done by if denied an iPod and a mobile phone. 'My parents had a vision for the future: we work hard now, we establish ourselves and we have a fine life', says Agnes, who would go to university to study social work and become a professional, as her parents had always wished, intent on giving her the opportunities denied them. This is what most parents want for their children, of course. For immigrant families the impulse shapes the struggle to get a foothold in a new land, imbuing the whole project with a purpose that puts hardships in perspective, not that many would stop to think about it. The idea that resilient people find meaning in the experience is regularly advanced, giving a bit of spiritual heft to the self-help parables that now guide us through the murk, while avoiding the unedifying fact that people intent on getting on with things are often the last to bother philosophising about it.

The Forbats would spend the next few years in a succession of rooms, surrounded by growing piles of garments, moving from the basement in Kings Cross to a two-room place above a hardware store in Bondi Junction, where Michael slept in the room that had the cutting table, to a full-sized factory, where they finally had their first dispatch room and office. By the end of the fifties, they were filling orders for many hundreds of garments a week, helped by maker-uppers, as outworkers were called then—migrant women from Greece and Italy, and later from China and Vietnam, plying their needles for the growing legions of tailors, hat-makers and seamstresses who'd arrived from the backblocks of Eastern Europe. Their ancestors had been identified with the clothing trades for two thousand years. The Jews who fled to Australia would be instrumental in the rapid growth of the ready-to-wear clothing industry.

Oblivious to the fact that we were playing a part history had ordained for us, I first heard the name Forbat when I was at school, because my mother did business with the company. I imagine I went to their factory. I worked in the shop on Saturdays and tagged along in the school holidays if mum was visiting her manufacturers, mostly dotted around Sydney's Central Station and neighbouring Surry Hills; I also went along once or twice to factories in Melbourne's Flinders Lane, most memorably in 1962 when we shared a railway sleeping car with two bunks and woke to find the uniformed guard, who had just knocked, setting down a breakfast tray with a flourish hardly merited by the contents of the tray: a pot of weak tea—English tea, my mother called it—a few bits of toast and an orange. We had been picturing something a bit more extravagant in the breakfast department. The contrast would have been enough to make my mother laugh. She could laugh at almost anything. If I think of her as she was almost to the end of her life, I can see her face folding into a look of helpless amusement.

Gratifying as it is to pay tribute to the spirit that kept her going eight or nine years after her heart surgeon told her she was surviving on will power alone (another feat of endurance that combined a high tolerance for pain with her habitual grit), there was nothing especially unusual about the life trajectory of one of countless thousands of survivors uprooted and tossed about like flotsam and jetsam before finding a home on the other side of the world. Indeed the 150 000 to 200 000–year history of human migration since our distant ancestors legged it out of Africa with big cats snapping at their heels seems to suggest that resilience may not be so unusual either, even if the American Psychological Association was having us on when it said, 'Resilience is not a trait that people either have or do not have'—again brushing over the inconvenient facts with the meliorist creed that resilience, like the Bronze Medallion or a St John Ambulance first-aid certificate, can be acquired in readiness for hard times. Of course an individual's capacity to withstand trauma and tragedy isn't as fixed and immutable as the tides. But that doesn't alter the fact that resilience is like an instinct in some people and not in others.

Ingrid Poulson's book *Rise*, published in 2008, is about developing some of the resilience Poulson herself showed after her estranged husband murdered her two small children and her father, then himself.[5] Poulson did not succumb to these horrors. *Rise* suggests the choices she made were what allowed her to bounce back, a reflection of the behaviourist dictum that people can choose how they respond to what happens to them, in that way creating who they are. I wouldn't wish to come off as the hapless determinist here, much less the helpless fatalist, but I feel compelled to point out that science said otherwise, even before 2003, when scientists matched genetic data against a large longitudinal study in Dunedin, New Zealand, to confirm what we surely already suspected: that genetics and environment between them may predispose a person to be more or less susceptible to what the researchers called 'environmental insults'.[6] They found that there are four variations of the gene 5-HTT, which is critical for the regulation of serotonin to the brain. While one form of the serotonin transporter gene protects people from depression if they experience stressful life events, the most common form of the gene has the opposite effect. But it doesn't cause depression on its own. The differences between people with different forms of the gene show up only in response to stressful events. Two in three people in the Dunedin study were in the group genetically predisposed to be vulnerable; one in three was in the group predisposed to be resilient, the category that would have included my mum.

Until the day she told me she had lost the will to live, my mother so thoroughly embodied resilience the attribute became blurred in my mind with other aspects of her temperament, like her tendency to make light of the things that had befallen her, her physical ailments included. In old age, she was a little taller than a garden gnome, with a broad back somewhat twisted by the curvature of her spine. She was still hailing buses with her walking stick when she was well into her eighties but, in the last year or two of her life, could go outside only with assistance, despite the walking frame. The crippling osteo-arthritis meant that almost any movement might hurt like the devil, not that she said much about it. Instead visitors would be struck by her spirit, contrasting her curi-osity and her openness to experience with the way old age had physically closed her in. My own view is that her resilience was paralleled by her ability to wring the best out of life. Ten months before she died, I drove to Canberra with her and her friend

Jacqueline Meredith. We were booked in at the Hyatt, where we had stayed earlier that year for her ninety-first birthday. My mother loved grand hotels. It pleased her to recall staying in the Hotel Metropole in Monte Carlo, or the Hotel Empereur in Maastricht, in the days she and my father travelled overseas every four or five years, another source of pleasure to her later on when those holidays had come to be emblems of a life well spent. By late 2006, it was difficult for her to leave her apartment at all. Even with the Zimmer frame, and her dear friend and me at her side, every step was something of a trial; we went in at the back of the hotel, where there weren't any stairs, and had very slowly proceeded to the lobby when my mother stopped still a moment, glancing about appreciatively before nodding to herself. 'I feel at home here', she said.

I suppose we were always close, though I had married and divorced and lived in New York City a long time, moving back to Sydney for my mother's sake in the last years of my father's life. He had become reluctant to leave their apartment. He wasn't ill but had grown so forgetful, after numerous small blackouts, that going out of doors may have made him feel disoriented or fearful. The differences between my mother and father were starkest when they reached old age. Until her mid-seventies, my mother continued to visit clothing manufacturers, doing the buying with the woman who had bought her shop, a role she gave up because she was worried about leaving dad on his own. What would happen to them a few years later happens to many elderly couples. One falls. The day comes when the other isn't strong enough to get him or her up and into bed again, and the ambulance is summoned in the middle of the night. There had been a few of these falls by the time the GP declared that my mother could no longer care for my father at home without one or both ending up in hospital with broken bones.

They had been married half a century, seldom spending a night apart, when dad left home in an ambulance for the last time. He was in hospital and then, very briefly, a nursing home before a stroke put him in hospital again. Given a small room in the grounds of the hospital, my mother spent most of the time by his side, in case he came to again, as he had the first day. My father had been devoted to my mother. Even in the last years, sunk into a vague sort of gloom, he brightened when she walked into the room. There may have been moments in the hospital he was aware of her presence, but it was distressing either way. I had never seen my mother so forlorn, because I had never before seen her defeated by circumstance. She was seventy-eight years old when dad died in January 1994. Once again, she dealt with her grief by making plans, declaring before long that she had decided to move closer to my brother and me because that would make it easier for us to visit her. Though her flat was listed with an agent, she sold it herself, afterwards delighting in the recollection that the buyer was a former customer who used to dither for hours over buying a skirt or blouse but took five minutes to choose a new home.

Before that had happened, however, my mother and I boarded a plane to Amsterdam, first stop on a month-long trip conceived as an interlude between the old life and the new. I remember isolated incidents from the weeks that followed. In Holland, we first drove south in a rented Opel and met up with the stout, white-haired matron who as a girl had helped my mother around the old farmhouse; as we walked towards the place, which now bore some kind of historical plaque, the two of them laughed over a memory of the day I was born. Kusters, the collaborator, happened to have reappeared a few hours later, in the mad hope of making another claim; egged on by mum, Dientje was upstairs, standing at the window of the bedroom with the heavy baby scales, ready to drop them on his head, but other neighbours chased him away. When my mother and I had come and gone from Holland and were in New York a few weeks later, sitting on a bench on the boardwalk at Coney Island with a friend of mine and her mother before eating borscht and blintzes at a Russian restaurant nearby, we saw a man—one of those

small, fastidious sort of men who somehow manage to marry women twice their
size—walking along trailing two jewelled
leashes behind him, blissfully unaware
that his two poodles had slipped the leash,
at least until our shrieks of laughter alerted
him. I remember the laughter, and I guess
that alone bodes well for my own resilience.
But the truth is that if I think back to that
trip, as we whirled from family visits in
Holland to family visits in Israel three or
four months after my father's death, I can-
not remember the signs of the raw grief
my mother must have felt. Memory plays
tricks, of course. If I look at photographs
of that time, I see her face was more drawn
than usual. In other respects, she was so
much like her usual self that it is only

now, looking back, that I notice I took her resilience for granted, carelessly assuming she would rise above the wish to have her suffering acknowledged, as she rose above the pain from her inflamed joints, to enjoy herself if she could.

It goes almost without saying that it is fortunate to be in the position to travel around the world to distract oneself from one's distress. But don't get me wrong: aside from her love of travel and hotels with more gilded plasterwork than Versailles, my mother was a woman of modest tastes, still wearing clothes from her shop twenty years after the shop had closed, and obstinately refusing to buy a new sofa in case she didn't get much wear out of it before she died, a sample of her own black humour that made her laugh time after time. The zest behind the humour was both the source of her resilience and the quality that gave her fortitude its sparkle. Like so many members of her generation, she was capable of enduring hardship without complaint, but there was nothing resigned about her. I suppose one was lucky to have dodged the English legacy that embraces misery like comfortable old clothes. Not one to go on about something as obvious as the fact that she missed my father, she took the opportunity to do things that had been more difficult when she was looking after him, going to more concerts and plays, even when climbing up and down theatre stairs became something of a trial. She was content with her own company, as long as she had a novel in her hands and some orchestral music on the radio, and in any case, kept herself diverted playing the stock market in a small way. Her eyesight wasn't up to much. Sometimes, if I let myself into her apartment, I would see her with the magnifying glass in one hand and her nose practically buried in the columns of figures in the business pages of the papers, looking up at me with a smile before announcing with satisfaction that she had just made several hundred, or a thousand, dollars.

But the pleasure she got from life was never the same after March 2003. A few days before the USA invaded Iraq on the flimsiest of pretexts, my brother and his family, my mother and I joined millions of people in antiwar rallies around the country and around the world. My mother, on a walking stick, couldn't go far. Jules would never protest again. He was on a cycling holiday with friends later that month when an accident left him severely brain-damaged. He was fifty-five. For the first time, I doubted my mother's capacity to emerge from a shattering crisis. I was too distraught to comfort her—and what was to be said, after all, to a woman of eighty-eight who would have wished herself dead many times over in place of a son reduced to such abject helplessness. He was in a coma for months, then in a rehab unit, then in a nursing home up the street from where he had lived but would never live again. He had been the capable sort, who would whip up a meal for friends or come and fix your computer if you called him, for he was always helping people; now his brain injury meant he couldn't help himself. He recognised his family and close friends, spoke a little in answer to questions and even learnt to write a word or two in big, childish letters with his left hand if pressed to do so.

I used to think that my mother had remained buoyant through much of her life because she had the capacity to keep some part of herself from being affected by all she had seen and experienced—almost as if the hardiness she had shown could be explained only by something a little impervious, like an extra membrane that protected her from being overwhelmed by grief and sorrow. On the other hand, like many members of her generation, my mother felt she should keep painful memories to herself, taking them out occasionally in private, like relics kept in tissue paper. But her grief could no longer be contained. One day she told me she often cried when she was alone, a heartbreaking admission that would have been unthinkable a few months earlier. Grief would also catch me unawares, tears spilling over at unexpected moments, when I was driving to work alone or listening to a piece of music on the radio.

In the instant my brother went over the handlebars of his bicycle, his life was destroyed and everything in our lives was turned upside down, which is what happens to families contending with calamity. His children had to look after the man who had looked after them. Their fortitude was enough to give me hope for the generation now entering public life, but even more notable was the strength my mother mustered at a time her body threatened to fail her altogether. She was like some character in a Beckett play, except that her body parts didn't fall off; they just stopped working one after another. When I think of the real test of her resilience, I think of those last years when she miraculously kept going because she was so worried about what would happen to my brother. Though she would never again recover the sheer effervescence that had been so typical of her vitality, the mixture of realism and adaptability that had let her take lesser setbacks in her stride asserted itself as we made practical arrangements. It was to her apartment that my nephew and I brought Jules two or three times a week, for the family meals my mother continued to cook until she could no longer pick up a pan.

My brother died in 2007. He had caught pneumonia a few weeks after his sixtieth birthday. His funeral was a revelation: four years after his accident, several hundred people turned up to remember him with real respect and affection. I had been aware that his death would mean my mother could let go, but it all happened with shocking rapidity. My mother fell a day after his funeral and was taken to hospital. At the end of the week, she told me she had lost the will to live. 'I lost my will', she said simply. When I brought her home from the hospital the following week and helped her to her usual chair, she picked up the remote and consulted Bloomberg for a few minutes before asking me to call her broker and sell two small parcels of shares she wanted out of her portfolio before she died. She faced death with equanimity. 'Don't wake me up', she told me, ten days later, at the end of the one day she had spent in bed. I asked her if she believed she was dying. 'Yes', she said, and we assured each other we were glad to be there together. My mother died a little over an hour later. I can't help thinking it's no coincidence the stock market tanked before a month was out, as if she had been holding it up by sheer force of will.

Notes

1 B Benard, *Resiliency: what we have learned*, WestEd, San Francisco, 2004.

2 A Deveson, *Resilience*, Allen & Unwin, Sydney, 2003.

3 D Coutu, 'How Resilience Works', *Harvard Business Review*, vol. 80, no. 5, May 2002.

4 A Siebert, solicited correspondence with *Harvard Business Review*, prior to publication of Coutu article, 11 April 2002, viewed online February 2009, <www.resiliencycenter.com/articles/hbresponse. shtml>.

5 I Poulson, *Rise*, Pan Macmillan Australia, Sydney, 2008.

6 A Caspi, K Sugden, TE Moffitt et al., 'Influence of Life Stress on Depression: moderation by a polymorphism in the 5-HTT gene', *Science*, vol. 301, 18 July 2003, pp. 386–9.

Acknowledgements

My heartfelt thanks to my friends Kathy
Bail and Helen Scott—for their gener-
ous help with this book and for much else
besides.

I received invaluable assistance from my
mother's friends and former colleagues
Jacqueline Meredith, Jenny Fallon, Joyce
Ludeke and Wendy Speziale, from my
brother's staunch friend Dr Leo van
Biene and from Professor Ian Hickie of

the Brain and Mind Research Institute at the University of Sydney.

I would also like to thank Foong Ling Kong, my publisher and editor at MUP, and copyeditor Lucy Davison.

Elisabeth Wynhausen is the author of *Dirt Cheap: Life at the Wrong End of the Job Market* and *Manly Girls*, a memoir. She was a journalist for many years and a senior writer for *The Australian* newspaper.